LET'S VISIT SCOTLAND

Let's visit
SCOTLAND

ANGUS MacVICAR

BURKE

First published April 1966
New edition October 1969
Revised and reprinted October 1976
Fourth revised edition 1984
© Angus MacVicar 1966, 1969, 1976 and 1984
All rights reserved. No part of this publication may be reproduced, stored in a retrieval system, or transmitted, in any form or by any means, electronic, mechanical, photocopying, recording or otherwise, without the prior permission of Burke Publishing Company Limited.

ACKNOWLEDGEMENTS

In collecting pictures for this book, the Author has been given generous and invaluable help by Ian McColl, editor of the *Scottish Daily Express*; Robert McKean, Scottish Manager of B.E.A.; W. M. Ballantine, Director of the Scottish Information Office; and Mrs May K. Brown, General Secretary of the Scottish Council of Physical Recreation.

The following firms and organizations spared neither time nor trouble in putting excellent photographs at his disposal: Colvilles Ltd., Motherwell; D. Johnston & Co., Islay; Jute Industries Ltd., Dundee; the Forestry Commission; the National Association of Scottish Woollen Manufacturers.

Other pictures have come from the British Travel and Holiday Association; Robert Estall; John Jochimsen; Geoffrey Kinns; John Leng & Co. Ltd.; A. D. S. MacPherson; the Royal National Life-boat Institution; Scotsman Publications Ltd.; the Scottish Development Agency; the Scottish Tourist Board; D. C. Thomson & Co. Ltd.; the United Kingdom Atomic Energy Authority.

To all these individuals and organizations the Author offers his sincere thanks.

CIP data
MacVicar, Angus
  Let's visit Scotland. – 4th ed.
  1. Scotland – Social life and customs – Juvenile literature
  I. Title
  941.1085'8   DA772
ISBN 0 222 01021 5

Burke Publishing Company Limited
Pegasus House, 116–120 Golden Lane, London EC1Y 0TL, England.
Burke Publishing (Canada) Limited
Toronto, Ontario, Canada.
Burke Publishing Company Inc.
Bridgeport, Connecticut, U.S.A.
Filmset by Green Gates Studios, Hull, England.
Printed in Singapore by Tien Wah Press (Pte) Ltd.

Contents

	Page
Map of Scotland	6
How Scotland Began	7
Landmarks in Scotland's History	13
Lovers of Freedom	18
Mountains and Cliffs	24
The Sea and Some Monsters	29
From Cattle-thieves to a Radio-tower	34
The Wild Things	38
Danger—Basking Sharks	44
Sailing Down the Clyde	47
The Forth and Edinburgh	53
Tweed from the Tweed	59
Jute, Jam and Journalism	63
Aberdeen and the North-east	68
Industrial Revolutions	73
The Church, Education and the Law	81
What Kind of People Are the Scots?	85
Index	95

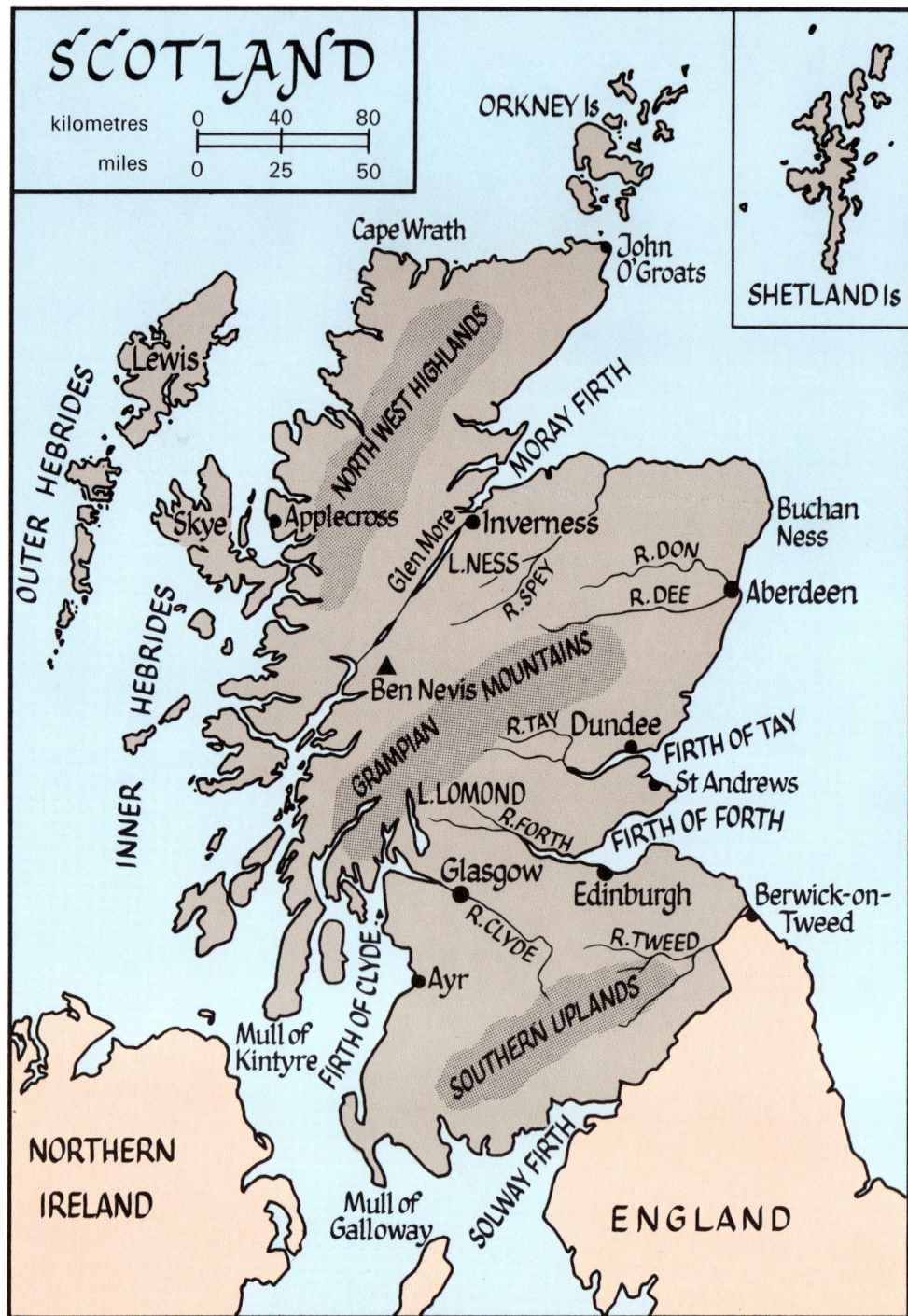

How Scotland Began

The first visitors to Scotland arrived some 8,000 years ago, crossing the sea from Ireland in small boats made of twigs plastered together with clay. They were men of the Stone Age, most of them very short in stature, dark-skinned and slant-eyed, with flint arrows and flint tools stuck in their belts of reindeer hide.

They found a land as empty of human life as the surface of the moon.

Before this time, for tens of thousands of years, the northern

Ben Nevis, the highest mountain in Britain

part of Britain had been covered by the cold of the last Ice Age. Dying volcanoes had become craggy, cold mountains like Ben Nevis in the west—at 1,342 metres (4,406 feet) the highest point in Britain—and Ben Macdhui (pronounced Mak-DOO-ee) in the north-east. Slow-moving rivers of solid ice, called glaciers, had scoured out deep valleys between the mountains. Then, as the snow and ice melted, avalanches of lava and mud had thundered down the crags. In the sheltered valleys a few patches of vegetation had begun to grow.

When the small men came, it was in the valleys that they settled, where they could get water from the rivers. At this time civilised people lived in other parts of the world—in Egypt and China, for example. But the small men were savages.

Centuries passed, and the Stone Age was followed by the Bronze Age. As the snow and ice receded still farther into the Arctic, the climate of northern Britain improved. The soil became more fertile, and animals and birds increased in numbers.

The first human visitors were joined by others from Ireland and southern Britain—wandering tribes whose arrow-heads, drinking utensils and primitive tools are still being dug up by archaeologists. Their "brochs", or stone houses, which were sometimes built partly underground, their forts and cairns and standing-stones can all be visited and inspected in almost every part of Scotland. The Clava Stones, near Culloden in Inverness-shire, provide a good example of a Bronze Age settlement. But all these tribes continued to live in separate groups, suspicious of each other, unwilling to share hard-won food and shelter with their neighbours.

The Romans invaded and conquered southern Britain in 55 B.C. In A.D. 80, Julius Agricola led his legions northwards into the rugged land which he called Caledonia (from the Latin, meaning "woodlands"). He pressed on as far as *Mons Graupius* (a name later corrupted to Grampius, from which the Grampian Mountains get their name). There he won a battle;

This Perthshire scenery makes it clear why Julius Agricola called Scotland *Caledonia,* meaning "woodlands"

but as a result the tribes became united for the first time and began to drive the invaders back.

They fought so fiercely that the Romans built two great walls to try and keep them in check. The first—known as Hadrian's Wall, after the Roman Emperor Hadrian—was erected between the River Tyne (now in England) and the Solway Firth. A second was put up, farther north, between the rivers Forth and Clyde. This one was called Antonine's Wall, after the Emperor Antoninus Pius. The remains of these huge defensive barriers can still be seen; but, in fact, neither proved much of an obstacle.

The Romans described the Caledonians as *Picti*, or Picts, "the painted people". It would seem, therefore, that they were in the habit of painting and tattooing themselves like the American Indians.

They were followers of the Druids, whose religious teachings were based on worship of the sun. The Druids also practised magic and made human sacrifices, and their influence was probably as strong and terrifying as that of the witch-doctor in more recent times. Groups of tall stones, said to be Druid "temples", remain standing today. Good examples are to be found at Stennes and Brodgar in Orkney, at Callanish, in the Hebridean island of Lewis, and at Dunadd, near Lochgilphead in Argyll.

But though the Pictish tribes—the forerunners of the Scottish clans—banded together to keep the Romans out of their territory, and though missionaries from southern Britain

The Maiden Stone, an early Christian monument in Aberdeenshire. Erected during the eighth or ninth century, it has a Celtic cross on one side and Pictish symbols on the other

and Ireland now began to spread amongst them the Christian gospel of brotherly love, the idea of forming themselves into a nation, under a central government, had not yet occurred to them.

St Ninian was the first Christian missionary to work amongst the Caledonians. He was probably a Pict himself, though educated in Rome. Around A.D. 397 he built his *Candida Casa* ("white house" in Latin) on the Isle of Whithorn in Galloway —an "island", by the way, which is really a peninsula. On the coast near by is a cave which he used as an oratory, or preaching-place, before erecting his stone chapel; and it was to Whithorn Priory that the Scottish kings made their pilgrimages for many centuries. In the museum at Whithorn and in the church at Kirkmadrine there are sculptured stones going back almost to St Ninian's day—stones which may be the oldest Christian relics of British origin.

St Ninian made many journeys into the east and north, and his influence was considerable; but after his death in A.D. 432 the Pictish tribes still remained disunited and suspicious of one another. In the meantime, a Celtic tribe called the Scots had been emigrating from Ireland to Caledonia and had now established themselves in the west. They spoke a language called Gaelic (pronounced GAH-lik), which still survives. The leaders of the tribe ruled wisely and encouraged the work of the Christian missionaries who followed them.

The most notable of these was St Columba, an Irish churchman, who has been described as "strong in stature, voice and spirit". With his disciples he founded a monastery in the island of Iona, off the coast of Argyll, which was a Druid stronghold. Indeed, almost every Columban church was built in a place where the Druids had formerly been established. An example of this occurs near the Mull of Kintyre, where a ruined Columban chapel is situated outside a cave containing a sacrificial altar. Historians are agreed that St Columba "built the new faith on the foundation of the old".

Like St Ninian, he journeyed widely throughout Caledonia. He was a statesman as well as a churchman, and his forceful yet kindly personality impressed the painted tribesmen. The influence of the Druids grew less strong as the Picts began to recognise the value of Christian neighbourliness, co-operation and love. The perseverance, over the centuries, of godly men and far-seeing tribal chiefs at last bore fruit.

In A.D. 574, the Scots came to an understanding with some of the Pictish tribes, and Aidan, then King of the Scots, was elected the first King of Scotland. He was crowned by St Columba in Iona; and it is believed that the Druidic Black Stone on which he sat during his coronation is the same Stone of Destiny on which the kings and queens of Great Britain are still crowned in Westminster Abbey in London.

From that moment, Scotland became a kingdom in her own right, with her capital at Dunadd, in Argyll.

Landmarks in Scotland's History

In King Aidan's time, Scotland was a small area in the west. Today (as shown in the map on page 6) the kingdom stretches from the lighthouse on Muckle Flugga in Shetland right down to the Solway Firth. (Muckle Flugga may sound like a swear-word, but it comes from the Norse and means, simply, "great rock".) Her boundary with England runs through the Cheviot Hills, from Gretna in the west to a point just north of Berwick-upon-Tweed in the east.

Scotland's size is 77,168 square kilometres (29,795 square

miles). The whole country is only a little bigger than the island of Tasmania and would disappear without trace in Lake Superior in North America. Her area includes 690 islands, 147 of which are inhabited.

An old legend in the Gaelic language tells that when God had finished making Britain, some fragments of earth and stone were left in His ample apron. With a smile He flicked them out, and they fell into the sea to form the islands of Scotland. A more modern legend has it that if the entire Scottish coastline were straightened out it would stretch from London to New York and back again, a distance of some 9,656 kilometres (6,000 miles).

The greatest length of the mainland, from Cape Wrath in the north to the Mull of Galloway in the south, is 490 kilometres (274 miles). The greatest breadth, from Buchan Ness in the east to Applecross in the west, is 297 kilometres (154 miles).

The most northerly part of the mainland is usually said to be John O'Groats House in Caithness. This is not strictly true. Dunnet Head, also in Caithness, extends a little farther north into the Pentland Firth.

John O'Groats was a Dutchman (John de Groot). He and his seven brothers were permitted to settle in Caithness during the reign of James IV (1488–1513). Their original house had eight sides, and their dining-table was also octagonal. This was because the de Groots could never agree as to which of them should occupy the front room or sit at the head of the table.

Caithness, though usually considered bleak and remote, has two claims to fame. Not far from Dunnet Head is the square and solid Castle of Mey, the Scottish residence of the Queen Mother. Only a little farther west, near Thurso, there has been built one of the most up-to-date buildings in the world—Britain's experimental fast reactor, a great ball-shaped structure at Dounreay (pronounced Doon-ray). By producing electricity, it helps to pay for itself; but its main purpose is to discover how best to get power from uranium rather than from coal. (The energy in one ton of uranium equals that in three million tonnes of coal.)

There are two other nuclear reactors in Scotland, one at

The Dounreay reactor

Hunterston in Ayrshire, and one at Chapel Cross near Annan in Dumfriesshire.

The present area of Scotland is the result of much fighting and argument throughout the past 1,400 years. Though the country was united and became a kingdom under Aidan, it was seldom at peace. The tribes, or clans, waged war amongst themselves. Invaders came from other lands and conquered parts of it.

Norsemen from Scandinavia (Norway, Sweden and Denmark) colonised Shetland and Orkney, the Hebrides and parts of the northern and north-eastern mainland. The magnificent, Norman-style Cathedral of St Magnus in Kirkwall, capital of Orkney, was built in the twelfth century in memory of a Norse king. The people of Lerwick, capital of Shetland, hold each January the Festival of Up-Helly-Aa, during which a full-scale model of a Norse galley, or long-ship, is dragged through the streets and finally destroyed in a bonfire made by the torches of its attendants.

Anglo-Saxons from Europe and Celtic tribes from southern Britain settled in the fertile, less mountainous lands in the east and south. The Celts were mainly Brythons, or Britons, whose legendary ruler was King Arthur; and it is said that Arthur's wizard, Merlin, lies buried in a mound at Drummelzier (pronounced Drum-EEL-yer) in Peeblesshire.

Eventually, however, the invaders were either driven out or absorbed into the Scottish population. In the reign of Malcolm II (1005–1034), the Anglo-Saxons and the Celtic settlers became subject to the Scots. In 1266, after a series of battles, the Hebrides were taken over by Alexander III from Magnus of Norway. Shetland and Orkney passed from Denmark to Scotland in 1468, as a pledge for the dowry of Margaret of Denmark when she married James III.

All this time, the Scots were fighting off attempts by the Angles, or English, to defeat them in battle and make Scotland a province of south Britain. Their resistance was as fierce as that offered by their Pictish ancestors to the Romans, for independence was—and still is—a strong characteristic of the Scots. Their national emblem is the prickly thistle. Their motto is *Nemo me impune lacessit*, which, in a rough translation from the Latin, means, "Nobody annoys me without getting hurt."

In 1297, William Wallace, a soldier and patriot, defeated the English at Stirling Bridge. On Abbey Craig, outside Stirling, from which Wallace controlled the battle, there now stands the towering Wallace Monument, built more than a hundred years ago. Inside it, a museum contains Wallace's "two-yard" sword. This famous weapon is, in fact, 1.67 metres ($5\frac{1}{2}$ feet) long and so heavy that its owner must have been very strong to wield it. Though victorious at first, Wallace was finally defeated by the English at Falkirk. He was captured and executed in London in 1305.

One year later, Robert the Bruce (an ancestor of Britain's present Queen Elizabeth II) was crowned King of Scotland. He inspired his countrymen to continue the fight for freedom.

The Lerwick festival of Up-Helly-Aa—a full-scale model of a Norse longship is being burnt on a bonfire

In 1314 he led them to a brilliant victory over the invaders at Bannockburn, also near Stirling. A statue of Bruce now overlooks the scene of the battle, one of the ten most decisive in history.

Lovers of Freedom

For two hundred years after Bannockburn, Scotland was at the height of her pride and power. In 1320, the Scottish clergymen and people sent a letter to the Pope, which contained the following sentences: "*While there exist a hundred of us, we will never submit to England. We fight not for glory, wealth or honour, but for that liberty [without] which no virtuous man shall survive.*" The letter was signed at the small town of Arbroath in the county of Angus and is sometimes called the Arbroath Declaration.

During this time, however, the kings and nobles of Scotland were mostly concerned with international politics and with keeping up the country's military strength. It was left to the Church, as so often happened, to help and encourage the ordinary people. The monks developed agriculture and industry and were the patrons of poets, painters and musicians.

Then came a succession of young, weak kings. The nobles began to struggle for power amongst themselves, and the tide of Scotland's greatness began to ebb. In 1513, James IV and

Highland cattle near Glencoe (Argyll)

his army were disastrously defeated by the English at the Battle of Flodden in Northumberland (England).

A famous song and bagpipe tune was composed about Flodden. It is a lament called *The Flowers of the Forest*, which describes how the young Scottish king and his soldiers—the "flowers of the forest"—were cut down and killed.

From then on, Scotland came more and more under the influence of England. In 1603, the Union of the Crowns took place, when James VI of Scotland, a son of Mary Queen of Scots and a great-great-grandson of Henry VII of England, was declared James I of Great Britain.

It took a long time to get all the clan chiefs to swear allegiance to a British monarch. Some of them had still not done so by 1691, and they were given until the end of December that year to comply. All the clans signed the document of allegiance except the MacDonalds of Glencoe (Argyll), whose chief was a few days late in reaching Inveraray. A punishment was prepared for them.

Early the following February, some 120 Campbell troopers under Campbell of Glenlyon, whose clan supported the British monarch, paid a visit to Glencoe. They came in friendship, they said, and were given hospitality by the MacDonalds. Then, in the small hours of the morning, they attacked their sleeping hosts, killing many men, women and children, turning the rest out to perish in the snow and burning their houses.

This was the infamous Massacre of Glencoe. Visitors to Glencoe today can see a memorial to the MacDonalds. Near by is the Signal Rock, from which the signal for the massacre was given.

Meanwhile, the Reformation was spreading. The man who did most to make Scotland a Protestant country was John Knox, who travelled everywhere preaching the new anti-papist doctrine. His body is thought to be buried in or near the High Kirk of St Giles in Edinburgh, and his statue now dominates the Assembly Hall of the Church of Scotland, also in Edinburgh.

The Scottish system of Protestant church government introduced by the Reformers is called Presbyterianism, because it operates through presbyteries, which are small local committees of clergymen and laymen. It is a democratic system differing from that in the Protestant Church of England, which is ruled from above by bishops appointed by the Crown.

For a long time the English tried to impose their system of bishops on the Scots, and this led to bitter quarrels and more fighting. But the Covenanters—so called because they signed a covenant or agreement to maintain their own form of worship—helped to keep the flag of Presbyterianism flying. It is still flying.

Towards the end of the seventeenth century, Scotland's economic position grew steadily worse, mainly because England refused to allow her free trade across the Border unless she accepted a complete union. In 1707, therefore, a Union of Parliaments was arranged. The union took place by no wish of the Scots as a whole, and its unpopularity led to rebellions in 1715 and 1745. These were known as the Jacobite Risings.

The Jacobites got their name from the Latin for James: *Jacobus*. They wanted to put the Scottish descendants of James I on the throne of Britain in place of George I, who, though also a descendant of James I, was German by birth.

The rebellion of 1715 petered out.

In 1745, however, Prince Charles Edward Stuart came across from exile in France, landed at Glenfinnan on the west coast of Inverness-shire and raised an army of the clans. He defeated the troops of George II at Prestonpans (East Lothian) and advanced into England.

But the clan chiefs were jealous of one another, and their jealousy resulted in bad team-work. They also neglected to provide their men either with sufficient food or with proper arms and equipment. The Jacobites were driven back and utterly routed at the Battle of Culloden near Inverness. Prince Charles Edward fled back to France.

The defeated rebels were cruelly dealt with by the King's soldiers—"Hanoverian red-coats" they were called, though a number of Scots were included in their ranks. Tortured, disarmed and put out of their homes, many Highlanders were forced to emigrate.

No one took much honour from the Jacobite Risings except the Scottish clansmen—the ordinary men and women who fought and died for a lost cause with the utmost loyalty and bravery. But the memory of "Bonnie Prince Charlie" lingers

Prince Charles Edward raised his standard here, at Glenfinnan

on in Scotland, particularly in the Highlands. Hundreds of songs and stories have been written about him. In Glenfinnan, where he first set up his flag, there stands a monument with an inscription in Gaelic, English and Latin.

Charles Edward was, in fact, a selfish and irresponsible young man, redeemed only by a certain charm of manner. To many Scots, however, his personal character is unimportant. For them he is a symbol of freedom—freedom to follow and enjoy their own particular way of life.

From the eighteenth century on, Scotland has been governed from London. People are inclined, therefore, to look on her as part of England. But the Scots will always regard themselves as a separate nation. At the Union of Parliaments they kept two institutions which are completely different from those of England—their Church and their Law.

Many Scots, indeed, hope that one day they may have their own Parliament again in Edinburgh; and, indeed, what is called a Scottish Assembly has been promised by all the political parties. Their promises have, however, not yet been implemented.

Mountains and Cliffs

In bygone ages, Scotland was the scene of mighty volcanic upheavals. The results are to be seen in the central Highlands and in the west and north, where the land is broken up into a confusion of mountains, gorges and deep lakes, or "lochs" as they are called by the Scots.

In sunlight the mountains seem richly clad in green, brown and white—the green of grass and pine-forest on the lower slopes, the brown of bare rock and heather in the higher regions, the white of snow on the peaks. When the mist comes swirling down, they have the appearance of haughty dames hiding behind scarves of grey gauze.

On a fine summer evening, the sight of the Cuillins (pronounced COO-lins) in the island of Skye is highly dramatic. They are the youngest mountains, geologically speaking, in Scotland, the remains of a terrace of lava broken down by

The Cuillins, the famous mountains of the Isle of Skye

glaciers. The highest peak, Sgurr Alasdair, soaring to 1,008 metres (3,309 feet), is flanked by castle-like towers, known as the Quirang and the Old Man of Storr. But facts like these give no clue to their savage beauty.

The mountains of Glen Torridon in Wester Ross present another notable picture. The sandstone of which they are formed glows red through the heather, and on their bare tops quartzite gleams like white icing on a cake.

Here in the north are many of the great deer forests of Scotland, though others can be found farther south. They are not, in fact, "forests" at all, in the usual sense of the word, but enormous tracts of empty moorland, where wealthy sportsmen, armed with rifles, hunt the antlered stags of the

Some of Scotland's most spectacular scenery is the result of mighty volcanic upheavals in the past

wild red deer. Centuries ago, Scotland is known to have been covered by scrub. Fossilised remains of trees are continually being dug up in marshland taken over by farmers or builders. This may be why the word "forest" is still used.

More magnificent scenery is provided by the Grampian Mountains (one of which is Ben Macdhui) and the Cairngorms. They are huge chunks of granite, thrust up by earthquakes through older rocks, and their tops are seldom free of snow; in recent years, some of the upper slopes have become fashionable ski-ing grounds. Snow-making machines are kept standing by, in case the weather is too mild! On the north-east face of Ben Nevis is the highest mountain cliff in Britain, with a drop of 457 metres (1,500 feet).

On St Kilda, in the North Atlantic, 84 kilometres (52 miles) west of Harris in the Outer Hebrides, is another breathtaking cliff, which plunges steeply into the sea. At one time

A ski-lift in the Cairngorms

some fifty people eked out a hardy, self-supporting existence on this remote island, with sea-birds as the main item in their diet. But in 1930 they were evacuated to the mainland, and now St Kilda is used for two oddly contrasting purposes. On the one hand, it houses a rocket-testing station. On the other, it is a strictly protected wild-life sanctuary, the breeding place of rare birds, including the St Kilda wren. It is also the home of a unique species of wild sheep, whose multiple horns and unfriendly habits are a frequent source of embarrassment to the soldiers guarding the rocket-station!

Another spectacular result of Scotland's geology is the waterfall in Sutherland called *Eas-Coul-Aulin* (pronounced Ace-cool-AH-lin), which is Gaelic meaning "the waterfall behind the lovely place". It has a total height of over 200 metres (658 feet) and is by far the highest waterfall in Britain. In the Kintail district of Ross-shire the Falls of Glomach also have a sheer drop. In sunlight their rainbow spray is magnificent. The Grey Mare's Tail in Dumfriesshire has a spectacular fall too.

The grandeur of Scottish scenery is associated in the minds of many visitors with the scent of peat-smoke. Peat is simply decayed vegetation, such as heather and moss, firmly packed under accumulations of soil. Layers of it are found all over Scotland, particularly in places where for thousands of years the land has been untouched by cultivation. It is dug up by thrifty farmers and crofters with sharp spades, cut into oblong blocks about the size and shape of building bricks, dried in the sun and wind, then stacked for use on household fires. The smoke has an aromatic scent and contains few of the unpleasant gases given off by coal.

The Sea and Some Monsters

Almost everywhere in Scotland the sound of moving water can be heard—the thunder of sea waves in a storm or their slow pulse on a white beach in calm weather; the hiss of rain on the surface of an inland loch or the lighter rustle as wind eddies over it; the surge of a mountain burn in brown spate or its gay rattle as it hurries along in more normal conditions, dark in its pools and glistening white amongst the rocks.

Except for her boundary with England, Scotland is ringed by the sea.

Harbours, fishing-ports, oil-jetties, shipbuilding and ship-breaking yards—and, in the Holy Loch near Dunoon, and at Faslane, nuclear submarine bases—are dotted around her coastline. The anchorage in Orkney called Scapa Flow is known to naval men everywhere.

Sea lochs thrust narrow fingers deep into Scotland, so that to reach a place only a short distance away by water, a very long journey by road is sometimes necessary. Ferry-boats, large and small, are fairly common—though not so common as they might be.

Off the east coast the sea is comparatively shallow and

chilled by Arctic currents; but the clear air and bracing weather of this area make it popular with holidaymakers, even though sometimes a clammy sea-fog, or "haar", comes creeping in from the North Sea. On the shores of the Moray Firth, where it is slightly warmer than elsewhere, grain and fruit crops ripen to the highest quality.

Off the west coast, the Atlantic is warmed by the Gulf Stream, a sea-current which drifts northward from the Gulf of Mexico. In this region, therefore, the weather is mild, though the mountains attract clouds and cause a heavier rainfall than in the east. From November to March the mean temperature in the West Highlands is higher than in the south of England. Every year certain plants used to be sent from Kew Gardens in London to winter out in the open at Inverewe (Wester Ross). They were returned, healthy and strong, in the spring.

Moisture in the Scottish air often results in gorgeous sunsets.

The Campbeltown life-boat going into action

The sky turns from gold and orange to pink and fiery red, and the scattered islands loom up against it on the horizon like sharply scissored cut-outs.

But at times the sunsets are hidden by dark storm-clouds. Workers out of doors lean into the rain and wind. Huge breakers crash down on the beaches and spout up against the cliffs. When this happens, the treacherous coasts are manned by coastguards, lighthouse-keepers and life-boatmen, all on the alert for trouble. From the grey Pentland Firth down to Berwick-upon-Tweed in the east and to the Mull of Galloway in the west every mile of coast has witnessed a shipwreck at one time or another.

The volunteer life-boat crews do splendid work, though to-day, thanks to radio beacons set at danger points, shipwrecks are less common than they used to be.

The most dangerous spot in the sea around Scotland is the whirlpool of Corryvreckan (pronounced Korrie-VRECH-kan), which lies north of the island of Jura near the Argyll coast. Corryvreckan is a Gaelic word meaning "the whirlpool of Breacan", and this Breacan appears to have been a Pictish chief who was drowned there. No small boat, however well built and engined, can sail near it except in a dead calm and at the right state of the tide. Even on a summer's day it boils like liquid in a pot; during a storm the water swirls so violently that it looks as if it were being sucked down into a pit. The whirlpool is caused by a meeting of several tides; but a Gaelic legend has it that beneath Corryvreckan lies the home of a sea-beast. Maybe this is where the wild sheep of St Kilda came from!

The majority of Scots have the sea in their blood. This is not surprising, because so many of them have been born and brought up within sight and sound of it and are accustomed to the taste of salt in the wind. They man the trawlers and the fishing-skiffs and the little steamers with brightly painted funnels which carry passengers, mail and cargo to all the islands. They join the Navy and the Merchant Navy; and it has been said that a Scots engineer can be found in almost every ship plying the oceans of the world.

The inland lochs vary in colour from silver and blue in summer to grey and muddy brown in winter. In sunlight they mirror the birch and pine woods, the mountains and fields and villages which surround them.

Of the freshwater lochs, tree-rimmed, island-studded Loch Lomond is the largest and, on account of the song bearing its name, the most famous. Lying between Dunbartonshire and Stirlingshire, it is the largest inland water in Britain, being 38 kilometres (24 miles) long and eight kilometres (five miles) broad.

The most interesting Scottish lochs are probably those in Glen More, or the Great Glen, which is the result of a geological fault reaching across Inverness-shire from the Moray Firth in the north-east to Loch Linnhe in the south-west (pronounced LIN-nie). This chain of lochs is linked by artificial waterways, the whole forming the Caledonian Canal.

Though not much used by larger vessels nowadays, the canal allows fishing-skiffs to get quickly from one coast to the other without having to make the long and sometimes dangerous passage around the north of Scotland.

The biggest and best known in the chain is Loch Ness, home of a fabulous monster. St Columba is supposed to have seen this monster and, by prayer, to have rescued one of his disciples from its clutches.

Indeed, since history began, frequent sightings of a creature in Loch Ness have been recorded. In recent years, tourists and natives (and the monks of St Augustus monastery) have seen— and photographed—something with a humped back, long neck and small head, which, from the descriptions given, bears a strong resemblance to a plesiosaurus. This prehistoric animal

Is this the Monster?

Loch Lomond—the largest (and perhaps the most beautiful) inland water in Britain

has been considered extinct for thousands of years; but then, so was the coelacanth, and not long ago specimens of this odd fish were discovered alive in the seas around Madagascar.

From Cattle-thieves to a Radio-tower

But of course Scotland is not one vast picture postcard of towering mountains, romantic islands and monster-haunted lochs.

There are the *machairs* (pronounced MACH-ars) of the

Hebrides and the west coast—sandy plains and tidal reaches on which grow the tough, salty grasses which are considered ideal food for sheep and beef-cattle. There are the rich farms of Aberdeenshire, Perthshire and Ayrshire, sheltered by trees and well watered by lazy streams. There are the low-lying lands on the east coast, where the county of Fife has been called "a beggar's mantle fringed with gold". The beggar's mantle part, in central and west Fife, includes bare farm-lands and coal-mines. The fringe of gold is a sandy coastline stretching from Aberdour to St Andrews, described by holidaymakers—and keen golfers—as "the Scottish Riviera".

The Lothians, too, around Edinburgh, are flat and fertile, rising gently into the rounded contours of the Lammermuir Hills to the south-east. When soldiers from England marched into East Lothian in the seventeeth century, they were astonished by the richness of the red soil, on which grew "the greatest quantity of corn they ever saw".

The Borders present yet another series of pictures, beginning with the gently undulating plain of the ancient Brythonic province of the Merse in the south-east.

To the south-west are the Lowther Hills, a "vast expanse covered with thick, short, tawny grass and moss". Here are the wild-fowl estuaries of the Solway coastline and the little fields of Galloway surrounded by stone walls, or "dykes" as they are called in Scotland. And here, too, are the districts of Eskdale, Teviotdale and Liddesdale, all made famous by stories recounting the adventures of the Border reivers.

A typical scene in the Border country

Reiver is the Scots word for "plunderer"—and plunderers those men were, raiding their neighbours and stealing cattle. The town of Jedburgh (Roxburghshire) gives its name to "Jeddart Justice", which means that a reiver when caught was hanged on the spot without a trial. The reivers were outlaws, bloodthirsty men riding on dark errands through the woods and dales; but as in the American "Wild West", where courage was a particular virtue, they became the heroes of innumerable ballads which are often sung even today.

Scotland is a kingdom with many aspects, some dramatic and beautiful, some monotonous and even drab; but everywhere man's enterprise is in evidence.

Aeroplanes drone overhead, leaving or approaching the many small aerodromes and the international airports which operate in Scotland—the latter at Aberdeen, Edinburgh, Prestwick (Ayrshire), and Abbotsinch, near Glasgow.

Towering piles of slag (the name commonly given to the refuse dug out along with coal) stand like pyramids near the pit-heads of the central industrial areas, though nowadays some of them are disappearing as the slag was used for bottoming roads and streets in "new" towns such as Glenrothes (Fife), Cumbernauld (Dunbartonshire), East Kilbride (Lanarkshire) and Livingston (West Lothian).

Railway lines, telegraph poles and wires, raw new roads and even soaring ski-lifts appear in improbable places, like crude pencil lines on a masterpiece of landscape painting.

Through corrie and glen, across moor, loch and mountain-

A British Caledonian plane, a familiar sight in Scotland today

side there march the giants of modernity—massive concrete pipes directing water-power to generating stations and tall steel pylons carrying the resulting electricity to town, village and factory, to castle, farm and isolated cottage.

In the centre of everything, half-way along the road between Edinburgh and Glasgow, at Kirk O'Shotts, there stand two great towers. They are the main distributing units in a radio and television network which daily supplies the country with news, comment and entertainment. On a lonely Highland moor a shepherd's family with a television set can watch a British monarch being crowned in Westminster Abbey and catch a glimpse of the Stone of Destiny tucked away beneath the throne. Enough to make King Aidan turn in his grave!

The Wild Things

The plant and animal life of Scotland has great variety, which is only to be expected in a country with twenty national nature reserves.

Most of the windswept islands are tree-less. So are the northern Highlands. But in the Lowlands there are lush acres of woodland, where alder and ash rub branches with oak, birch and beech. The crab-apple tree and the rowan, or mountain ash, grow wild everywhere. It is rowan and crab-apple jelly which gives a royal flavour to soda scones—a speciality of the Scottish housewife.

In the mild west, palm trees can be found growing alongside subtropical shrubs like fuchsia and rhododendrons, while in the central areas elm and hazel stand shoulder to shoulder with poplar, sycamore and yew.

All over the country, State forests of pine, fir and larch blanket the lower slopes of the mountains. This is the result of good work by the Forestry Commission, a Government body

A State forest of larch

which has done much to help unemployment in Scotland. Many more forests are still being planted, ensuring a supply of wood for future building and paper-making.

At Culbin, near Forres (Morayshire), the Commission has planted a forest on a vast area of drifting sand which was threatening to smother the farmlands. Representatives from various countries interested in forestry and soil reclamation make regular visits to study the work being done there.

Wild flowers bloom everywhere in Scotland, from Alpine saxifrages on the mountain-tops to buttercups in the low-lying fields, from foxgloves in the woods to wild violets on the *machairs*. Heather grows plentifully, too, giving the countryside its typical purplish colour in the autumn.

The national policy of creating nature reserves has been a boon not only to young hikers looking for fresh air and

Spraying some of Scotland's precious trees with insecticide—Culbin Forest

exercise away from the big cities but also to the wild birds and beasts of Scotland. When old forests were cut down by commercial concerns eager for building material and by landowners making room for sheep, many birds and animals were deprived of their natural cover. Now forests are being planted again, and the wild population is increasing.

Native Scottish birds include the magnificent golden eagle, the ptarmigan and the red grouse. Pheasants and partridges scuttle through the heather and the turnip-fields, and swans sail gracefully on many of the lochs. Buzzards hover above the wooded hills waiting to swoop on the first rabbit or squirrel that moves on the ground below. Like the golden eagle, the buzzard is a member of the hawk family. While hovering, it has the appearance of being "stuck" in the sky.

For a long time the chough (a kind of crow) and the osprey were in danger of dying out in Scotland. Now, however, thanks to devoted work by naturalists, choughs may be found nesting in the islands and ospreys are breeding again in the Cairngorms.

In the autumn, when Arctic birds are migrating southwards, Scottish bird-watchers have the time of their lives. Some Arctic species, such as the barnacle goose, actually spend the winter in the Hebrides.

St Kilda has the biggest colony of gannets, though other gannetries occur around the coast, notably on the Bass Rock in the Firth of Forth and on Ailsa Craig in the Firth of Clyde.

The gannet, or solan goose, is one of the most interesting of

Scottish sea-birds. It has a wing-span of about 1.8 metres (six feet), eyes like telescopic lenses and natural shock-absorbers in its neck. It certainly needs them. Its method of securing a meal is to fly slowly at a great height—often well over thirty metres (one hundred feet)—then, when it spots a herring in the sea below, to plummet down and grab it, entering the water with the speed of an express train. Sometimes, a flock of hundreds of gannets can be seen, feeding on a herring shoal. They hurtle down in a black and white shower, sending up spouts of spray as they crash into the water. Then they bob to the surface again, clumsily swallowing their catch in two or three gulps before flapping heavily skywards for another dive. The excitement of such a scene is tremendous.

Besides the native red and roe deer, Scotland has herds of fallow deer and Japanese sika deer. In the rutting (mating) season the belling, or roaring, of the red deer stags can be heard all over the Highlands. At one time deer were killed in hundreds for food and for sport. Now stag-hunting is controlled.

Hares have become a pest since the rabbit population was reduced by the deliberate spread of the disease called myxomatosis. Otters, stoats and weasels are common in Scotland, and badgers and wild-cats still roam the lonelier parts of the countryside. The wild-cat is seldom seen; but when disturbed it can be fierce and dangerous. People walking on the moors must also be wary of the adder. This is a small snake about the size and shape of an eel, with a dark zigzag marking down its back from head to tail. It can move quickly, and its bite is poisonous.

Foxes exist in fair numbers in Scotland, and there is some fox-hunting on the English pattern, with horses and hounds. This is mainly in the Lowland counties. Elsewhere foxes are shot like hares and other vermin.

At sunrise on a cold, calm winter's morning the grey Atlantic seals come up on the Scottish sea-rocks. They sprawl and puff and stretch, balancing on their stomachs with heads and tails arched upwards, for all the world like huge birds. Though called grey, they vary in colour. The nearly three-metre (nine-foot) bulls are sometimes olive brown, like sea-weed, or they may be dark iron-grey. The cows have coats the colour of slate, with irregular black spots showing through. The calves have white fur, like small polar bears.

Most of the world population of Atlantic seals breed in the

Wild cats, like this one, are still found in lonelier parts of the countryside

waters around Britain—mainly in the Hebridean islands of Rona and Hasgeir (pronounced HAY-skir). A professional salmon-fisher hates the sight of them. Sometimes they raid his nets at the river-mouths and eat parts of his catch. About eighty per cent of their food consists of salmon. As a result, clubbings and shootings are continually going on in an effort to control their numbers. Yet grey seals are friendly in a way that is almost human. A picture to warm the heart is that of a white-furred calf playing alone at the bottom of a sea-pool, curiously turning over stones and shells.

Danger—Basking-sharks

Around the Scottish coasts fish are plentiful. Herring, cod, mackerel, plaice, sole, haddock and whiting appear on every breakfast-table. Crabs, lobsters and prawns are common. But Scotland has one sea creature she could well do without. This is the basking-shark.

Fishing-skiffs have been damaged, small boats sunk and men drowned as the result of encounters with basking-sharks. On a quiet, moonlight night in the fishing-grounds, fishermen often watch them leaping as high as 4.5 metres (15 feet) out of the water. The crash of their falling bodies can be heard far away. They do not deliberately attack a boat but are dangerous because of their contrary nature. When their snouts touch anything they immediately lunge ahead, straight into the obstruction.

Sail-fish, as they are sometimes called, grow to over 15 metres (50 feet) in length. A specimen has been caught with a powerful, perpendicular tail three metres (ten feet) high. Their colouring is grey rather than black, with a whitish stomach which is usually blotched with black patches and old wounds or scars. They have wicked little eyes near the end of a square snout.

When a shark's lower jaw hangs open, the inside of its mouth gleams like the white enamel in a bath. The teeth are small, because its food is the same as that of the herring— masses of tiny shrimps called plankton which swim near the surface of the sea in calm weather.

A fisherman is afraid of basking-sharks because they follow the plankton in the wake of the herring shoals and so run

Loch Eck (Argyll)—the home of the powan and the charr

foul of the skiffs. Their feeding habits account for their name. When their three big, sail-like fins stick up out of the water, they are not really basking in the sun at all—they have come up to browse on the plankton. They appear off the coasts of Scotland in April and remain there until late autumn. Generally they move about in groups of four; but shoals of about fifty have been seen in the Minches, between the Outer Hebrides and the mainland.

For the amateur fisherman, Scotland is paradise. The number of lochs and streams is almost beyond reckoning, and salmon, sea-trout and brown trout are abundant. The powan

Fishermen checking their nets in Lerwick Harbour. Fishing is an important industry in North East Scotland

is a rare fish which can be found in Loch Lomond and Loch Eck (Argyll). It is a member of the salmon family, and is sometimes mistakenly called "the freshwater herring". A unique sub-species of charr also lives in Loch Eck.

Scotland's wild life reflects the land itself—beautiful yet often savage, friendly but at times withdrawn. Her domestic plants and animals come into a different category.

Sailing Down the Clyde

The great rivers of Scotland are of vital importance to the well-being of her people.

The entire population of Scotland is only about 5,250,000—far less than that of Tokyo, London or New York. But at least half of this number live in and around Glasgow, whose own population is 855,000. The reason for this is mainly the River Clyde, with its wide, sheltered approaches and the deposits of coal and iron along its banks.

The Clyde is over 170 kilometres (106 miles) in length. Its source is a tiny spring in the Lowther Hills in south Lanarkshire. At first it ripples along among quiet hills, farms and orchards. On its right bank, stretching away to the east, are the sheep farms and grain farms of the Lothians. On its left bank, lie the dairy farms of Lanarkshire and Ayrshire.

Ayrshire became prosperous in the nineteenth century

through coal-mining. Many of the coal seams are now running out. But the county is still prosperous enough, chiefly because of its efficient modern farms and the modern light industries being established in, for example, the new town of Irvine.

At one time the ladies of Kilmarnock carried on a brisk trade in "Kilmarnock bonnets", which they knitted in their own homes. This quaint form of Scottish headgear was like an outsize beret, with a red "toorie", or pom-pom, on top. It is seldom seen nowadays; and Kilmarnock has become noted instead for its carpet-weaving. Heavy boots for miners and farm-workers used to be made in Maybole. Now the individual shoemakers have been replaced by shoe-factories. Prestwick has an aircraft industry. This was developed in connection with the international airport there, the most fog-free one in Britain.

On the coast is the town of Ayr. It was here, seven hundred years ago, that William Wallace started his War of Independence by setting fire to "the Barns of Ayr", knowing that English soldiers were billeted inside. Here Robert the Bruce held a parliament in 1315 to decide who should succeed him as king. Today Ayr has a large holiday camp, a race-course and a dozen first-class golf-courses near at hand.

Ayr's chief pride, however, is Robert Burns. Just to the south, in the village of Alloway, is the thatched cottage in which Scotland's greatest poet was born in 1759.

The Clyde rises in the fertile countryside of south-west Scotland. The first signs of industry occur at the Falls of Clyde,

A photograph taken in a modern electronics factory in Livingston—
a "new" town in West Lothian

near the town of Lanark, where its waters are harnessed to a hydro-electric supply. Then it begins to run through a busy area containing enormous steel-works, iron-works and tin-plate works in Motherwell, Coatbridge and Airdrie. A little farther on, the Clyde enters Rutherglen, which claims to be older than Glasgow and, in typical Scottish fashion, refuses to amalgamate with the city.

At last the river comes to Glasgow Green, the park where Prince Charles Edward reviewed his army in 1745. Here it becomes a part of Glasgow, the biggest and the oldest city in Scotland.

Glasgow's patron saint is Kentigern (otherwise known as Mungo, "the beloved"). He settled in this area in A.D. 543; but there was a settlement by the Clyde before that, and the place was visited by the Romans. The beautiful and dignified Glasgow Cathedral was built in 1124, and a University was established in 1451. The present University is a more modern building dating from 1870, pleasantly situated on one of Glasgow's many hills.

In the eighteenth century, the author of *Robinson Crusoe*, Daniel Defoe, described Glasgow as "the most beautiful little city in Europe". In the twentieth century, John Betjeman, the

Glasgow Cathedral, built in 1124

The fourth great Cunard liner, the *Queen Elizabeth II*, being built on Clydebank

English poet and writer, has called it "the finest Victorian city in the world".

In its centre are many fine office buildings, solid blocks of nineteenth-century stone standing cheek by jowl with ultra-modern skyscrapers of concrete and glass. In some districts broken-down old tenements are still occupied; but these are gradually disappearing and new houses going up in their place. The rents of most new houses are subsidised.

As it flows through Glasgow, the Clyde becomes a harbour with a huge area of docks. Big ships sail right into the heart of the city. An enormous sum has been spent in deepening the river—there is a saying among Glaswegians, that "Glasgow made the Clyde, and the Clyde made Glasgow". Bridges and tunnels carry ceaseless traffic from bank to bank.

Beyond the docks, on either side, are the shipbuilding yards, whose tall, hammerhead cranes look odd against a background of woods and hills. During the Second World War more ships were launched in the Clyde than in all the shipyards of America put together.

On the northern bank is John Brown's (now owned in part by an American company) which built the battleship *Vanguard* and the four great Cunard liners. Hereabouts the Clyde is so narrow that these vessels could not have been launched at all, were it not that the mouth of the River Cart is opposite John Brown's. After launching, they crossed the river diagonally so that their sterns went up into the Cart. Today, instead of liners, the yard constructs rigs and accommodation modules for the oil companies.

Clydebank's neighbouring town, Dumbarton, continues the pattern of brisk industry. Shipyards, factories and oil-depots jostle each other for breathing-space. Beside Dumbarton Rock, which towers high above the river like a miniature Gibraltar, a huge distillery makes whisky from grain.

From here on, the Clyde begins to widen. The town of Paisley on the left bank is noted for its thread mills and for the local manufacture of marmalade and jams. On the same side, in Port Glasgow and Greenock, are more shipbuilding yards. From Port Glasgow, in 1812, the first practical steamship in Europe was launched by Henry Bell. This was the *Comet*, a full-scale model of which can be seen in the town. Greenock has the oldest shipbuilding yard in existence—Scott's, built in 1771. It also has sugar-refineries and a firm which manufactures the "big tops" for many famous circuses.

South of Greenock, the river estuary is called the Firth of Clyde. Fishing ports and holiday resorts are set around it like jewels. Through it the big ships sail out past the lovely islands of Bute and Arran, past the Heads of Ayr to port and the ancient volcanic rock called Ailsa Craig to starboard. Then they swing north under the cliffs of the Mull of Kintyre and finally west again into the Atlantic.

During the past century, the Clyde has been identified with heavy industries like steel, shipbuilding and engineering. Now the picture is changing and many light industries are being established along its banks, particularly in the new towns and industrial estates near Glasgow.

The Forth and Edinburgh

Edinburgh, though less commercial than Glasgow, has grime, too. This has given it a nickname—"Auld Reekie", reek being the Scots word for smoke. On the whole, however,

Auld Reekie. A view of Princes Street

the capital city of Scotland is a beautiful place and has been called "the Athens of the North". At its centre is a great rock, 133 metres (437 feet) high, on which stands a castle, visible from every corner of the city. On one side the rock is so sheer that it has been scaled only three times in history. Another landmark within its boundary is a hill called Arthur's Seat. Who Arthur was remains a mystery, though it may have been King Arthur of the legend.

Edinburgh is built on the southern shore of the Firth of Forth. The Forth rises west of Stirling and flows for 106 kilometres (66 miles) into the North Sea. For 85 kilometres (53 miles) it is tidal—a fact which helped Robert the Bruce to win the Battle of Bannockburn. East of Stirling it is bridged three times—by a road bridge at Kincardine-on-Forth, and by a new road bridge and an old railway bridge standing alongside each other at Queensferry.

The Queensferry road bridge, which was once the longest suspension bridge in Europe, is a masterpiece of engineering. It was opened by Queen Elizabeth II in 1964 and lets motor traffic from the north come directly into Edinburgh. It has a single span of 1,005 metres (3,300 feet) and a total length (over water) only 30 metres (100 feet) less than the Golden Gate in San Francisco, U.S.A.

The railway bridge, opened in 1890, is another notable example of Scottish engineering. Built on the cantilever system, its only foothold from shore to shore—a distance (over water) of 2,527 metres (8,291 feet)—is the tiny island of

An aerial view, showing the new Forth road bridge on the left and the older railway bridge on the right

Inchgarvie (once fortified against Paul Jones, the pirate) which supports its central pier.

Before reaching Queensferry, the Forth passes on its south bank an industrial area centred on Falkirk and Grangemouth.

Falkirk's prosperity was based on iron-works; and at one time it was the scene of cattle fairs called the Falkirk Trysts. Here William Wallace was defeated by the English in 1298. Just outside its boundary are a few remains of Antonine's Wall.

Since the Second World War, no Scottish town has expanded more quickly than Grangemouth. It has a huge crude-oil refinery, chemical and engineering works, docks and shipbuilding yards. An electronics industry has now been established in the same area.

On the north side of the river, the ancient and Royal Burgh of Dunfermline stands just inland. Dunfermline Abbey, founded in the eleventh century by Malcolm III (1057–1093), is famous as the burial-place of seven Scottish kings, including Robert the Bruce. (Malcolm III, by the way, was called Canmore, which is from the Gaelic, meaning "big-head". The nickname appears to have referred to the actual size of his head, not to any delusions of grandeur he may have had!) Andrew Carnegie, the American millionaire noted for his philanthropy, was born in Dunfermline, and the various charitable trusts founded by him have their headquarters in the town. Its main industry is the manufacture of linen.

A little further east along the same bank of the river is a big Naval Dockyard at Rosyth.

Edinburgh (population 467,000) and its port of Leith lie beyond the Queensferry bridges. They owe their size and importance to the fact that, through the ages, merchants sailing in from northern Europe to do business with the Scots found the Firth of Forth a safe and convenient landing-place.

Being the capital, it is not surprising that Edinburgh should be like a tapestry, reflecting in detail the whole history and life of Scotland.

West of the High Kirk of St Giles, built into the causeway in stones of a different colour, is the picture of a heart—"the Heart of Midlothian". This marks the position of an old building called the Tolbooth, where Scotland's parliaments used to assemble. South of St Giles is Parliament House (containing the Law Courts), where much of Scotland's legal business is carried out.

Kings and queens lived in the Palace of Holyroodhouse, which lies at the foot of "the Royal Mile", the Castle being at the other end. In the Castle are kept the Crown Jewels of Scotland. Here, too, built on the exposed rock, is the magnificent Scottish National War Memorial. It displays books, open to inspection, in which are written the names of all Scottish service people (men and women) who died in the First and Second World Wars.

On the George IV Bridge is the Scottish National Library, and near by are the University buildings. Some distance away, in Waterloo Place, is St Andrews House which contains the various departments of the Secretary of State for Scotland.

The Palace of Holyroodhouse where the Kings and Queens of Scotland lived

   Three of the city's main industries are printing and publishing, brewing and the manufacture of glassware.
   Princes Street gives Edinburgh much of its beauty and character. It has only one side, made up mainly of shops. The other is open, with a view across Princes Street Gardens to the Castle. On this side there stands a monument to Sir Walter Scott (1771–1832), Scotland's most famous storyteller and author of *The Heart of Midlothian*. In Princes Street Gardens can be seen an enormous floral clock. This operates close to and parallel with the ground and keeps perfect time. The hands and figures glow brightly with living flowers.

Tweed from the Tweed

The River Tweed is 156 kilometres (97 miles) long. It rises in south Peeblesshire and flows east through or between the counties of Selkirk, Roxburgh and Berwick, then between Berwick and Northumberland, where it forms the Scottish border. Finally it enters England and reaches the sea at Berwick-upon-Tweed.

The seaport and holiday town of Berwick-upon-Tweed is officially English; but its professional soccer team, Berwick Rangers, plays in the second division of the Scottish League! Because of its position on the main line of communication between the two countries, it was fought over for centuries, until in 1482 it finally became a part of England. After the Union of the Crowns, however, it seems to have been looked upon as a kind of "no man's land", because old documents often refer to "England and Scotland and Berwick-upon-Tweed".

The rolling, tree-clad countryside watered by the Tweed saw many a bitter skirmish between the Scots and English. It was later the happy—or unhappy—hunting-ground of the reivers. But during the reign of David I (1124–1153) it also witnessed the foundation of four great abbeys—at Melrose, Dryburgh, Jedburgh and Kelso. Today these are all in ruins. Melrose Abbey is the best preserved and has some finely carved stonework. In Dryburgh, situated amongst trees in a crook of the Tweed's arm, Sir Walter Scott lies buried. It was the monks connected with such places of Christian worship who, against all odds, developed the agriculture, industry and various arts which still flourish on or near the banks of the Tweed.

There is no iron or coal in the Borders, and the Industrial Age left this part of the Scottish Lowlands almost untouched. Its prosperity is founded firmly on wool. The gentle hills have always provided good sheep-runs; for centuries, the sheep's wool has been woven into cloth called tweed. Oddly enough, "tweed" is not derived from the name of the river. It is a corruption of the word "tweel", or twill, which describes a certain type of cloth.

To begin with, tweed was made by weavers working in their own cottages, as still happens in the Hebrides, home of the famous "Harris" tweed. Later, however, mills were estab-

Schoolboys learning to fish in the River Tweed

Weaving tweed, the modern way

lished in such towns as Hawick, Galashiels, Walkerburn and Innerleithen, and individual weavers were taken on as factory hands. Nevertheless, the mills produced cloth which retained much of the quality and sense of design of the original craftsmen. Today, using imported wools in addition to the local variety, the Border mills are known throughout the world for their output, which includes knitted as well as woven goods.

Dior, the Parisian fashion expert, helped to design some of the modern "knitwear".

The towns of Tweedside have annual festivals which are held only in the Scottish Lowlands. These are the traditional Common Ridings.

The Common Riding at Hawick is an example. Here a "Cornet" is elected. On the Friday after the first Monday in June, carrying the "Colours", or flag, he leads his men on horseback round the town's boundary (called "the marches" in Scotland), usually at a good gallop. Afterwards members of the company "buss", or kiss, the Colours at the "Teribus" Memorial in the High Street. Early next morning they climb the Moat Hill (from the Anglo-Saxon word "moot", meaning "a meeting place"), where they sing an ancient song called *Teribus ye Teri Odin*. The meaning of such words is obscure, but they are thought to be an invocation of Thor and Odin, ancient gods of the Norsemen. The "Teribus" Memorial consists of a horse and rider modelled in bronze. It was erected to the memory of the "callants", or young men, who captured the English Colours during a local skirmish in the sixteenth century.

The Anglo-Saxon and Norse influences in this old custom provide still more evidence of the mixed ancestry of the Scottish people.

Jute, Jam and Journalism

The longest river in Scotland is the Tay (188 kilometres (117 miles). It comes out of Loch Tay at Kenmore, in central Perthshire. At Ballinluig it is joined by the Tummel. Thereafter it runs by Dunkeld and Perth into a pot-bellied Firth, flowing at last into the North Sea by way of Dundee and the great bridges.

The new Tay road bridge

When Queen Victoria sat in her carriage she could see a vast panorama of Scotland from this point. Now it is called Queen's View

The Tay railway bridge is the third longest in the world, having 3,136 metres (10,289 feet) of waterway. The new road bridge, which links up with the new Forth bridge, has 2,194 metres (7,200 feet) of waterway.

The young life of the Tay is spent in a countryside made up of mountains and woodlands, lochs and lush green fields. It is a land of heart's desire for visitors and fishermen, as well as a rich farming and fruit-growing area. Here are many places made notable in song and story.

There is the Queen's View near Pitlochry, where Queen Victoria sat in her carriage and smiled down at a vista of her beloved Scotland. There are the Falls of Tummel and the Black Spout waterfall on the same river. A little north of Pitlochry there is the Pass of Killiecrankie, scene of a battle between Royalists and Covenanters in 1691. Graham of Claverhouse, otherwise known as "Bonnie Dundee", won the day for the Royalists at the cost of his own life. At the top of the pass is the Soldier's Leap, where a fleeing Royalist is said to have cleared the River Garry in one tremendous bound. Were he alive today, this man would surely break the world record for the long jump!

The Tay is fished for salmon by both amateurs and professionals. Today, sportsmen pay fabulous rents for the best "beats"; but salmon were once so plentiful in the Tay that farm-workers refused to sign on unless their employers promised to serve only one meal of salmon per week!

On its tributary, the Tummel, a big salmon-ladder has been

A view of Perth, on the River Tay

built, 274 metres (900 feet) long and with thirty-five pools. From a glass-sided observation-room underneath one of the pools, visitors can watch the salmon leaping as they climb to the spawning-beds. This ladder was made possible through the development of a great hydro-electric scheme, which created an entirely new stretch of water called Loch Faskally.

When it reaches Perth, the Tay leaves its sporting youth behind and begins to shoulder the burdens of industry. Perth is not only a road and rail junction but also, in a small way, a port. Its cattle markets are famous. Buyers from both North and South America and the Commonwealth regularly visit the "Perth Sales" to purchase beef cattle for breeding purposes. The chief industries of Perth include brewing, distilling and dyeing, as well as the manufacture of linen and glass.

The town is sometimes called "the Fair City", and its fine buildings, riverside parks and graceful bridges make it worthy of the title. Its old name was St Johnstoun (St. John's Town). This is echoed in the name of its ancient church, St John's (probably founded in Pictish times), where, in 1551, John Knox preached a violent sermon during his Protestant campaign. Incidentally, Perth's professional soccer team is called St Johnstone.

Scone (pronounced Skoon) is now part of Perth; but once it was the capital of Scotland. The Stone of Destiny was taken to Scone from Iona, and Scottish kings and queens were crowned on it until Edward I of England carried it off to Westminster Abbey.

Dundee (population 192,000) gives the Tay its industrial importance. It is said to have been founded on the three J's—jute, jam and journalism.

Jute is the fibre of an Asian plant used in the manufacture of things like coarse sacking, mats and rope. In its raw state it is shipped mainly from Pakistan, unloaded at Dundee's great dockyards and processed in the mills. The jute manufacturers have had an influence on civic affairs, and much of the city's prosperity and cultural life has resulted from their efforts, combined with those of the civic authorities. The new Queen's College, for instance, part of the University of St Andrews, is one result of their active co-operation.

Jam and other preserves are made in Dundee because of the big fruit-growing areas around Tayside.

Great numbers of journalists are employed here by Thomson-Leng. This printing and publishing firm produces all kinds of papers and magazines, including many "comics" known to children the world over. "Thomson-trained" journalists are as common as Scottish ship's engineers. They can be found in publishing houses everywhere.

Today, however, Dundee concerns itself with more than the three J's. Textiles, electronic products, engineering components and confectionery are all manufactured in the area. In the past, wealthy Dundonians invested a great deal of money in the cattle-lands of the American south-west. Now the Americans are returning the compliment by establishing light industries in the city—such as the making of clocks and cash-registers.

Dundee is in the county of Angus. So is the small town of Kirriemuir, famous because it is the birthplace of Sir James M. Barrie, author of *Peter Pan*. Many of Barrie's stories tell of life in "Thrums", with its dour brand of religion. Thrums is, of course, Kirriemuir; but the word also means "the loose ends in weaving", a reminder that the town was once noted for fine hand-made cloth.

Not far from Kirriemuir is Glamis Castle (pronounced Glams). This ancient building is the home of the Earls of Strathmore. Queen Elizabeth the Queen Mother, a daughter of the fourteenth earl, was brought up in Glamis, and Princess Margaret was born here.

Aberdeen and the North-east

The River Dee is 140 kilometres (87 miles) long. It rises in the Cairngorms and runs eastward past Braemar, Balmoral, Ballater and Aboyne. Its valley is known as "Royal Deeside", because long ago Queen Victoria and her husband, Prince Albert, chose it as their Scottish home. They bought Balmoral

Balmoral Castle built by Prince Albert

estate, which includes an enormous deer forest, and built Balmoral Castle, where the present Royal Family still go for holidays.

This whole countryside is littered with castles. It was the home-base of great clans like the Gordons, the Forbeses, the Frasers and the Farquharsons. They squabbled amongst themselves but often joined forces to fight for a national cause. From this region came many of the keenest Jacobites.

The Dee waters an area of good farm-land. Here the well-known Aberdeen Angus black cattle are bred and reared, as well as many thousands of sheep. Oats, barley, wheat and potatoes are also grown. The best of the barley goes to the making of whisky in the numerous distilleries of the north-east.

Finally, the Dee enters the sea by way of Aberdeen (population 220,000). This beautiful city always impresses a visitor with its freshness. There are no smoking factory chimneys, and the grey Aberdeenshire granite of which it is built sparkles bright and clean. Most of the granite comes from Rubislaw Quarry, now disused, which is so deep that it looks as if a mountain had been pulled out of the earth like a tooth.

Aberdeen is actually built on two rivers, the Dee and the Don. This may account for its odd name. "Aber" is simply the Gaelic for "on", but "deen" looks like a compromise!

Recently, off the north-east coast of Scotland, many oilfields have been discovered under the sea. As a result, Aberdeen has become the centre of a great and powerful oil industry. Its population now includes a great many businessmen and technicians from America and other foreign countries.

Aberdeen's harbour (recently reconstructed to accommodate the oil-men) and its busy fish market are in the new town at the mouth of the Dee. Soon after sunrise on a summer's

The River Dee which waters acres of good farmland

Pony-trekking in Inverness-shire

morning, a visit to the fish market is an exciting adventure. The sight and smell of thousands of fish—common and uncommon—being dumped on the quays, the rattle of winches and the shouts and jokes of auctioneers and buyers all combine to produce a lively and dramatic effect.

This is the centre of the great fishing industry of the north-east. Everywhere along the neighbouring coasts are fishing towns like Lossiemouth, Buckie, Peterhead and Fraserburgh. At one time they depended chiefly on their catches of herring. Now, as in Aberdeen, white-fishing plays a big part in their economy.

Besides oil and fish, Aberdeen's chief industries include the tourist trade, quarrying, engineering, shipbuilding and paper-making. There are also textile mills which produce tweed and knitted goods of high quality.

Another north-eastern river is the Spey. It is the fastest in Scotland and probably the most beautiful. From tiny Loch Spey in the foothills of the Monadhliath Mountains (pronounced Moan-a-LEE-ah), it runs for 177 kilometres (110 miles through the glens, rocks and pinewoods of Inverness-shire, Banffshire and Moray. Along its banks are hotels and hostels catering for fishermen, mountain-climbers, skiers, pony-trekkers and golfers. It provides power for electricity and water for the making of whisky. At Fochabers (Morayshire) a food and canning industry has been established. This makes use of the plentiful supply of fish and game in the district.

Not far from the mouth of the Spey is Inverness (population 31,400), sometimes called "the capital of the Highlands". In 1723 Daniel Defoe reported that "they speak as good English here as in London". Today the people of Inverness still have a clear and pleasant accent. This may be because their English is spoken alongside Gaelic and is an acquired rather than a native language.

The manufacture of tweed is carried on in the town; but its main industry is tourism. Inverness has a long history of association with royalty. King Brude of the Picts lived in a castle nearby, where he entertained St Columba. MacBeth, about whom Shakespeare wrote his play, owned a castle in the town. So did Robert the Bruce; and Prince Charles

Edward stayed in Inverness before the Battle of Culloden.

Beyond the towers of the Cathedral of St Andrew is Tomnahurich (pronounced Tom-na-HOOR-ich). This small hill has an interesting legend attached to it.

The story goes that it marks the burial place of the *Feinn* (pronounced Fane), three giants of ancient Scotland. A bugle was buried with them, and it was prophesied that if the bugle were blown three times the *Feinn* would rise and free Scotland from her oppressors. One day, many centuries ago, a curious boy found an opening in the hill and went inside. He saw the bugle and blew it, not once but twice. To his horror he saw three huge figures stirring in the dark and rising on their elbows. He dropped the bugle and fled, and no one has ever found the opening again.

According to the legend, therefore, the *Feinn* are still there, resting on their elbows, waiting for the third bugle blast to summon them to the aid of their country.

Industrial Revolutions

For more than two hundred years Scotland has been governed from London. She is now represented in the British Parliament by seventy-one members, and the Scottish Office, occupied by the Secretary of State for Scotland, is in Whitehall.

The four administrative departments of the Secretary of

State are in St Andrews House, Edinburgh—the Department of Agriculture and Fisheries for Scotland, the Scottish Education Department, the Scottish Home and Health Department and the Scottish Development Department.

The Home and Health Department needs some explanation. It deals with the Scottish police and the probation service, with criminal justice and legal aid, with Scottish prisons and Borstal institutions. It is the central authority in Scotland for the fire service and civil defence and on the law relating to shops, theatres, cinemas and licensed premises. It is also responsible for the administration in Scotland of the National Health Act, including the hospitals. It looks after the aged, the handicapped and the war pensioners.

Many Scots believe that government from London is a bad thing, because officials in Whitehall may often be ignorant of local conditions. To support their claim, they point out that Scotland has always had a higher proportion of unemployed people than England. The Scottish Development Department, however, has done much to improve the situation; and the Highlands and Islands Development Board will continue to do still more. The third bugle blast at Tomnahurich may not be required for some time yet!

One of Scotland's greatest problems has always been the movement of people away from the land, especially in the Highlands. This began after the Jacobite Rising in 1745, when farmers and crofters who had supported Prince Charles Edward were brutally expelled from their homes. Those who were left had their rents increased. Between 1763 and 1775, about 20,000 Highlanders emigrated to North America.

Another upheaval took place at the beginning of the nineteenth century. The Napoleonic Wars raised the price of wool, and sheep became more profitable than cattle. Landowners decided to get rid of their crofting tenants and turn their estates into huge sheep-farms. Mass evictions were organised, known as "the Clearances". If the crofters refused to leave, soldiers were sent to burn their houses. Some who tried to resist were killed. Others died of starvation. Many were forced to emigrate; so that today, in Canada, America, Australia and New Zealand, there are hundreds of families whose ancestors left Scotland because of "the Clearances".

Early nineteenth-century Scotland was like Europe after the Second World War; refugees sought desperately for work and a place to live.

Some of the evicted crofters drifted south and were lucky enough to find employment in Glasgow and Edinburgh. The same kind of thing is still happening, though country people now go to the big cities by their own choice. Most of those who go to the cities are young, attracted by what they believe to be a more exciting way of life. Recently, however, instead of excitement, most of them have found unemployment.

At one time farming in Scotland—as in the whole of Britain—was neglected. Butter, cheese, meat and bacon, all heavily subsidised by overseas governments, poured into the country. The prices obtained by home producers fell almost to starvation level. In 1930, for example, Scottish dairy farmers were getting minimum prices for their produce.

Finally, the Government in London realised that farmers would have to be protected and encouraged, because in the event of war the country might have to depend for food almost entirely on its own resources. Boards were set up to market farm produce on a co-operative basis. This helped farmers to compete profitably with their overseas rivals, and when the Second World War did break out, they were ready to make a big production effort. Since then, the introduction of subsidies, guaranteed prices, improvement grants and loans has brought about a complete revolution in the farming industry.

At the turn of the century Scottish farmers were in the peasant class. Now many own their own farms and have a high standard of living.

Even on crofts too small to provide a man with a decent living for his family, conditions have improved. This is largely due to the work of the Crofters' Commission, which operates under the Department of Agriculture and Fisheries. Crofters receive a variety of grants and are encouraged to develop sidelines such as hand-loom weaving and letting rooms to summer visitors. The Harris tweed and Fair Isle knitwear industries were established by crofters working in their own homes.

Scotland's other ancient industry, fishing, also became more prosperous thanks to financial and scientific aid from the Government. But since the advent of the European Common

The Scottish tweed and knitwear industries were originated by crofters working in their own home. This crofter's wife is using a traditional spinning-wheel

Market, and the invasion of the fishing-grounds by European competitors, some Scottish fishermen are finding life bad again.

Much of the romance in Scottish farming and fishing has given way to efficiency. Combine harvesters have displaced the scythe. Radar-like echometers are now used, instead of long wires, to locate the herring-shoals. Yet some old shepherds still count their sheep in what they call fairy language, the numbers up to seven being "yan, tan, tethera, pethera, pimp, hothera, lothera". And fishermen still put a wreath of rowan twigs on the bows of their boats to bring them luck. Scholars reckon that the "fairy numbers" may be the last surviving examples of the old Pictish language. The rowan twigs are a reminder that the rowan tree was once held sacred by the Druids.

Though the drift from the land in Scotland has slowed down,

and farming remains reasonably prosperous, the problem of unemployment in the thickly populated areas has become serious. This is because yet another important change is taking place in Scottish industrial life.

Such changes have happened before. Two hundred years ago the economy of Scotland was based principally on the tobacco trade. Huge imports of tobacco from America meant that many home-produced goods could be exported in exchange. But when the American colonies broke away from Britain in 1783, this outlet for Scottish goods disappeared. Enterprising Scots industrialists, however, soon turned to the manufacture of cotton, which sparked off a new phase of activity. Then, around 1860, the American Civil War broke out. The cotton trade collapsed in its turn. This was when the heavy industries were fully developed; and once again Scotland became busy in coal-mining, steel-making and shipbuilding.

Then the mines began to run out. Foreign competition in steel-making and shipbuilding became stronger. The steel and shipbuilding bosses, in co-operation with the trade unions representing the workers, carried out successful programmes of modernisation. Nevertheless, Scotland gradually entered a further stage in her industrial history.

Her prosperity became more dependent on new light industries. With Government encouragement, car factories were built at Linwood (Renfrewshire) and Bathgate (West Lothian). The new pulp mill at Fort William (Inverness-shire)

The combined stacker/reclaimer at the Hunterston iron ore terminal —part of the steel industry modernisation programme

and the aluminium works at Kinlochleven (Argyll) and Invergordon (Wester Ross) gave employment to thousands of country people in the Highlands.

Older industries, such as printing, paper-making, linoleum, brewing and distilling, took on a new lease of life. Whisky, indeed, was Scotland's biggest dollar earner.

The Laphroaig Distillery on the Isle of Islay

But now, on account of the discovery of oil and of the new economic policies applied by Government, the situation is changing again. The car factory at Linwood, the pulp mill at Fort William and both aluminium works have all closed down. The distilling industry is contracting.

What does the future hold for Scottish industry? Answers may be found in the ubiquitous silicon chip and in the oilfields still to be discovered around the coasts.

The Church, Education and the Law

In politics, the majority of Scots vote Labour, though some farming counties generally return Unionist (Conservative) members to Parliament. Throughout the northern counties there is a strong Liberal tradition and support is also given to the new Social Democratic Party (SDP). The Scottish National Party (SNP) now campaigns not for complete separation from England but for a Scottish Parliament (or Assembly) in Scotland.

Scotland prides herself on being democratic. There is some class-distinction but not a lot. A colour-bar is unknown. Foreigners are given a genuine if sometimes cautious welcome and usually find the Scots good neighbours.

The Church of Scotland is democratic, too. Every clergyman is equal, and there is no head man like the Archbishop of Canterbury in the Church of England. Ministers are not placed in churches—each congregation chooses its own. Every year a General Assembly of ministers and laymen is held in Edinburgh. This is presided over by a Moderator who, after only twelve months in office, returns to his congregation.

The Church has had lapses from democracy. At the time of "the Clearances" a number of ministers took the side of the landowners, because it was the landowners who paid part of their "stipends", or salaries. This was one reason for the Disruption in 1843, when some members broke away and founded the Free Church of Scotland.

John Knox's house in the Royal Mile, Edinburgh

Today, like industry, the Church is faced with the problem of unemployment and a drifting population. In the country districts there are too many churches; in the new housing areas too few. But the difficulty is gradually being overcome.

John Knox, "father" of the Church of Scotland, was more than a churchman. He was also a schoolmaster. It was he and his Reformers who said there should be "a school in every town and a schoolmaster in every parish", so that all children, rich or poor, might have an education "according to their capacity". For a long time this democratic ideal was opposed by the nobility and the big landowners, who were afraid that servants and labourers would be hard to find if too many people were educated. But in 1872 the Education (Scotland) Act was passed and education became the responsibility of the State rather than the Church. Since then the vision of the Reformers has become an established fact.

The great majority of Scottish children now go to State-owned schools. There are less than a dozen "public schools" on the English pattern. Every sixteen- or seventeen-year-old who passes in a sufficient number of subjects in the "Higher Leaving Certificate" is entitled to a grant allowing him or her to attend a university. (Scotland has eight universities.)

One weakness in Scottish education is that it caters primarily for children in the industrial areas. If more could be done to educate country children for a country life, this might, in a small way, help to ease the unemployment.

The University of Glasgow was founded in 1451, Aberdeen in 1494 and Edinburgh in 1582. In 1964 the technical University of Strathclyde was established in Glasgow; and a new University has now been opened near Stirling. Within recent years, Queen's College, Dundee, separated from St Andrews and is now a University in its own right.

St Andrews University is the oldest. It was founded in 1411. The red-gowned students are an important part of the life of the old town, which has been a Royal Burgh since 1140.

The fame of St Andrews is due to history, religion and golf.

The tradition is that St Regulus (otherwise known as St Rule) landed here from Europe in the fourth century with some relics of St Andrew—"an arm-bone, three fingers, a tooth and knee-pan". Since then Scotland's patron saint has been St Andrew and her flag the white, diagonal St Andrew's Cross on a blue background. Every year, on November 30, Scots all over the world celebrate St Andrew's Day. They play bagpipes, dance Scotch reels, drink whisky and eat haggis. (Haggis is not an animal but a kind of pudding made of minced liver, suet and oatmeal. And, believe it or not, MacHaggis is a Scottish family name!)

At the time of the Reformation, two leading Covenanters, Patrick Hamilton and George Wishart, were burned at the stake in St Andrews, and here Cardinal Beaton was murdered in revenge. Here, too, in the early sixteenth century, golf was played on the sandy, wind-blown links between the River Eden and the sea. Today, St Andrews' "Royal and Ancient" is the world's leading golf club, and the Old Course is loved and respected by golfers everywhere.

Like her Church and educational system, the law of Scotland differs from that of England. It is based on principles of Roman law. The Court of Session is the highest civil court. Most civil cases—and a great number of the less serious criminal cases—are tried in local sheriff courts by a sheriff. The High Court of Judiciary is the highest criminal court. Its seat is in Edinburgh, but the judges also go out on circuit to other towns.

Most lawyers agree that the Scottish system of allowing lay magistrates to try certain cases is inferior to the English system. Punishments for similar offences are apt to vary too much. On the whole, however, the law of Scotland is careful of the rights of the individual. No evidence is made public until a man is finally tried. "Not proven" is a Scottish verdict unknown in England. It amounts to an acquittal. Anyone who has stood trial for a crime on which a verdict of "not proven" is returned cannot be tried again for that crime.

Her Church, her system of education and her law have kept Scotland from becoming a mere province of England. At the same time, it should be remembered that the Church of Scotland—even with an adult membership of about 1,000,000—is not the only Church of importance in the country. The Roman Catholic Church is strong, especially in the industrial areas. Its members are under the care of two archbishops and six bishops. The Episcopal Church, now in full communion with the Church of England, has many members who are English people living in Scotland. The Free Church has a large following in the Highlands and Islands. Nonconformist churches, too, are well attended.

What Kind of People Are the Scots?

There is no such thing as a typical Scot. He can be small and dark, like the little men who came from Ireland 8,000 years ago. He can be lean and red-haired like the painted Picts. He can be stout and strong like the Brythons and the

Anglo-Saxons. He can be tall and fair like the Norsemen. Or he can be a mongrel: a mixture of everything!

Neither is there a typical Scots accent. Highlanders have a musical lilt in their speech. Lowlanders are broad and deliberate. Glasgow has an accent all its own—a mixture of Irish and Lowland Scots—which is often as difficult to make out as London Cockney.

As for character, the Highlanders are supposed to be either gay and energetic or sad and lazy, according to their mood. The Lowlanders and east-coasters are supposed to be dour and hard-working, tight-fisted and lacking in humour. This is misleading. Highlanders can be dour and Lowlanders gay, and east-coasters can be full of fun. In the Hebrides, however, where there are no trains to catch, it must be admitted that nobody pays much attention to the clock!

Some visitors are warned to expect bagpipes and kilts at the back of every ben, and meanness in the heart of every Scot. This also is misleading.

Scotland has many fine pipers, trained as a rule in regimental bands; and among the hills and glens pipe-music can be enjoyed in its natural setting—the open air. But pipers are as numerous in other countries—Canada and India, for example, where pipe-bands are enthusiastically supported.

Scots do wear the kilt, including many "country gentlemen" educated at English public schools. But far more kilts are to be seen in England and abroad, worn by individuals who would like to be known as Scots. As far as working people are

Scottish pipers at the Royal Braemar Gathering

concerned, the climate of Scotland is a bit chilly for a garment like a short skirt!

Scots meanness is a music-hall joke started by the Scots themselves. They are, in general, a thrifty race, as the result of much poverty in the past. They are also kind to visitors. This is something that was handed down by St Columba, who wrote a poem called *The Rune of Hospitality*: "Give to the Stranger all thine house. Put food in the eating-place, drink in the drinking-place. For the lark sings in her song, 'Often, often, often comes the Christ in the guise of a Stranger'."

The chief characteristic of the Scot is probably independence. At times this makes him appear boorish and aloof; but underneath he is eager for company. He likes nothing better than a lively party, or *ceilidh* (pronounced kay-ly), as such a gathering is called in the Highlands. The people of the cities—especially Glaswegians—are sharp and humorous and noisy.

Gaelic was the language of the tribal Scots, including King Aidan and St Columba. It has much in common with Irish Gaelic, Cornish and Breton. For hundreds of years it was the language not only of the people but also of the Scottish court. Nowadays it is spoken in Scotland by only about 75,000 people, mainly in the Highlands and Islands—and in Glasgow.

Efforts to preserve it are being made. It is taught in some schools. Every year a National Gaelic Mod or Festival (corresponding to the Welsh Eisteddfod) is held in one of the cities or towns. Unfortunately, Gaelic has no business value and so is dying out as a spoken language. But, as with Latin, its store of beautiful literature will go on living, preserved by the work of translators. Its music has already become part of Scotland's heritage.

This music is generally for voices, and choirs are as plentiful as in Wales. Gaelic dance music is played as much on the violin (or fiddle) as on the bagpipes. Sometimes it is rendered by a single voice. This is called *puirt-a-beul* (pronounced poort-a-BALE), or "mouth-music".

An important Scottish event is the Edinburgh International Festival, which includes the Edinburgh Film Festival. This takes place every year in the early autumn. Here the native arts of Scotland can be compared with the finest drama, poetry and music in the world.

On the "fringe" of the Festival, jazzed-up folk music is

played and sung in cafés, bars and cellars, where young people drink coffee, dance, present plays and argue about many things until the small hours of the morning.

Scotland's best-known early poets, or "makars", such as Robert Henryson and William Dunbar, were of the same period as Chaucer—the late fourteenth and early fifteenth centuries. The spirit of democratic freedom was evident in all their writings. Though a poet of the Court, Dunbar wrote with understanding about the rights of the peasants.

Independence and a sympathy with ordinary people also inspired the poetry of Robert Burns (1759–1796), as is shown in *A Man's A Man For A' That*. His work is admired not only in Scotland but throughout the world. Only the Bible and Shakespeare have been translated into more languages. Another reason for his popularity is the warmth of his love songs. *My Love Is Like A Red, Red Rose* has been described as the most beautiful love song ever written.

Burns is sometimes called "the ploughboy poet". He was, in fact, extremely well educated, with a knowledge of Latin, Greek and the literature of other countries. He had many love-affairs, drank too much whisky at times and failed as a farmer. But he was never afraid to admit his faults and had a deep feeling for the sadness and joy of his fellow-men.

Sir Walter Scott's style of writing may be somewhat boring to modern readers. His sentences are long and involved, and he uses hundreds of words in describing even the smallest incident. But that was the style of his time. The plots of his

The cottage in Alloway where Robert Burns was born in 1759

stories are exciting and his characters brilliantly drawn. This has been proved in the radio, television and film versions of his novels.

He himself was an admirable character. As a successful writer of poems he lived in style. Then suddenly disaster came. His partner and publisher went bankrupt, and Scott was left penniless and in debt. But he wasted no time in self-pity. He settled down to work as he had never worked before, and during the next few years he produced many of the Waverley Novels, paid off his debts and became independent again.

From 1821 until his death in 1832 he lived in the mansion of Abbotsford, near Melrose, in Roxburghshire.

Like Scott, Robert Louis Stevenson (1850–1894) was a poet as well as a novelist. *Treasure Island* and *Kidnapped* are amongst the best known of his books, especially to young people. A visitor to Inveraray (Argyll) can see the old courthouse which gave him the idea for *Kidnapped*. Here James Stewart of the Glen was tried in 1752 for the murder of Colin Campbell ("the red fox") of Glenure. He was almost certainly innocent; but the judge and eleven of the fifteen jurors were Campbells, who hated the Stewart clan, and he was condemned to death.

The Scots have always been fond of arguing. It is not surprising, therefore, that the country has produced some notable thinkers, amongst them John Napier (1550–1617), the mathematician who invented logarithms; David Hume (1711–1776), the philosopher and historian, and Adam Smith (1723–1790), who is famous for his writings on economics and philosophy.

Scottish scientists and men of medicine include John Hunter (1728–1793), the pioneer of scientific surgery; James William Simpson (1811–1870), who first used chloroform as an anaesthetic, and Alexander Fleming (1881–1955), the discoverer of penicillin.

Today science and medicine are combined in the Air Ambulance Service run by Loganair for the Hospitals Board. This excellent service enables a patient from a remote Hebridean community to be flown direct—and without payment of any kind—to a Glasgow hospital. Many lives have been saved by "the Mercy Flight".

Scotland has a great engineering tradition. Thomas Telford (1757–1834) built the suspension bridge across the Menai

An air nurse—part of the Air Ambulance Service

Straits, while John MacAdam (1756–1836) invented a new method of surfacing roads. James Watt (1736–1819), famed for his part in the production of the steam-engine, was also a Scot. In the nineteenth century David and Robert Napier founded the Clyde shipbuilding industry.

Other famous and inventive Scots include Kirkpatrick MacMillan (1810–1878) who made the first bicycle; John Boyd Dunlop (1840–1941) who pioneered the air-filled rubber tyre; Alexander Graham Bell (1847–1922) who emigrated to America and gave the world the telephone; and John Logie Baird (1888–1946), the inventor of television.

Scotland's two leading explorers were Mungo Park (1777–1806) and David Livingstone (1813–1873). Park explored West Africa and the River Niger. Livingstone was a missionary. He travelled amongst the tribes of Central Africa in much the same way as St Columba had done amongst the Picts.

The best known of all Scottish sportsmen was probably Eric Henry Liddell who, in 1924, won a gold medal in the 400 metres at the Paris Olympic Games. His best distance was the 100 metres; but because the heats in this race were run on a Sunday, he refused to take part. Scotland's pride in his moral and physical courage was so great that his welcome back to Edinburgh was far warmer and noisier than the reception given to sportsmen today.

Sport in Scotland is taken almost as seriously as religion. In spite of Saturday afternoon television, soccer still attracts fairly big crowds. Fans of teams in Glasgow, Edinburgh, Aberdeen and Dundee travel all over the country to see them play. It is unfortunate that in Glasgow the Protestant supporters of Rangers should so often be at loggerheads with the Roman Catholic supporters of Celtic.

Hampden Park in Glasgow is the largest football stadium in Britain, and the record attendance there is 150,000. Strangely enough, Hampden belongs to Queen's Park, the only amateur team playing in a British senior league.

Rugby football in Scotland is completely amateur. It has its own following, particularly in the Borders; a crowd of 80,000 will gather at Murrayfield, Edinburgh, for an international match.

The old Scottish game of shinty—a kind of free-for-all hockey—is still played, mainly in the Highlands. The stick

Dancers at the Highland Games in Inverness-shire

used is called a *caman*. It can be swung to any height and in any direction, which results in plenty of bumps and bruises.

Golf is now the most popular game played by individual Scots. In every other house there is at least one bag of clubs. Courses are crowded, especially at week-ends. The spectators who watch championships at St Andrews, Turnberry and Troon are said by playing professionals to be the most knowledgeable and appreciative in the world.

Highland Games are held every year in many parts of Scotland. Pipers and dancers are all dressed in tartan. Athletes run, jump, throw hammers and toss trunks of trees, called cabers, which are sometimes more than six metres (twenty feet) in length. The spectacle is colourful and exciting.

In their various activities, the Scots are romantic as well as democratic. They like going to social and sporting gatherings as well as to church. They are rebels as well as patriots. To understand them better, a visitor should remember two things —the Arbroath Declaration, written in 1320 after the Battle of Bannockburn, and St Columba's *Rune of Hospitality*, written in the sixth century when Scotland first became a nation.

Index

Aberdeenshire 35, 69, 70, 71, 82
Aidan 13, 16, 38, 88
air ambulance 91, 92
airports 36, 48
Alexander III 17
Antonine's Wall 10, 56
Arbroath Declaration 20, 94
Argyll 10, 12, 13, 29, 31, 47, 79
Arran 53
Arthur, King 16, 54
Ayrshire 16, 35, 36, 47, 48, 53

Balmoral 68, 69
Banffshire 72
Bannockburn 18, 19, 54, 94
Barrie, Sir James 68
Ben Macdhui 8, 26
Ben Nevis 8, 27
Berwick-on-Tweed 13, 31, 59
"Bonnie Prince Charlie" *see* Stuart, Prince Charles Edward
Bronze Age 8
Bruce, Robert 17, 18, 48, 54, 56, 73
Brude, King 72
Burns, Robert 48, 89
Bute 53

Cairngorms 26, 41, 68
Caithness 14, 15
Caledonian Canal 32
Cape Wrath 14
Charles Edward Stuart, Prince 22, 49, 73, 74
Cheviot Hills 13
Church 21, 24, 81, 82, 84, 85
"Clearances" 75
Clyde, River 10, 41, 47, 48, 49, 50, 51, 52, 53
coal 15, 35, 37, 47, 48, 78
Covenanters 21, 65, 84
crofters 75, 76
Cuillins 24
Culloden 8, 22, 73
Cumbernauld 37

David I 59
Dee, River 68, 69, 70
Dounreay 15
druids 10, 12, 77
Dumfriesshire 16, 28
Dunbartonshire 32, 37, 52
Dundee 63, 67, 68
Dunfermline 56

East Kilbride 37
East Lothian 35
Edinburgh 21, 23, 24, 35, 38, 53, 54, 56, 57, 74, 75, 82, 88-9, 93
education 74, 82, 83
Elizabeth II, H.M. Queen 17
Elizabeth, Queen (Queen Mother) 15, 68

Falkirk 17, 56
farming 28, 35, 38, 47, 48, 64, 65, 68, 74, 75, 76, 77
Fife 35, 37
fishing 32, 44, 46, 47, 64, 65, 70, 71, 72, 74, 75, 76, 77, 78
Flodden 20
forestry 39, 40, 41
Forth, River 10, 41, 54, 55, 56, 64

Gaelic 12, 23, 28, 31, 57, 72, 88
Galloway 11, 14, 31, 35
Glasgow 37, 38, 47, 49, 50, 51, 53, 75, 82, 86, 91, 93
Glamis 68
Glencoe 20
Glenrothes 37
Grampians 9, 26
Grangemouth 56
Greenock 53

Hadrian's Wall 10
Harris 27, 60, 76
Hawick 62
Highlands and Islands Development Board 74

Ice Age 8
Inverness-shire 8, 22, 32, 72, 78

95

Inveraray 20
Iona 13, 66
Irvine 48

Jacobites 22, 69, 74
James III 17
James IV 14, 20
James VI 20, 22
John o'Groats 14
Julius Agricola 9

Kilmarnock 48
Knox, John 21, 82

Lammermuir Hills 35
Lanarkshire 47, 49
law 24, 84, 85
Lewis 10
Livingston 37, 49
Loch Linnhe 32
Loch Lomond 32, 47
Loch Ness 33
London 13, 18, 24, 73, 76, 86
Lowther Hills 35, 47

MacBeth 72
Malcolm II 16
Malcolm III 56
Margaret, H.R.H. Princess 68
Mary, Queen of Scots 19
Melrose 59, 90
Moray Firth 30, 32
Morayshire 40, 71

oil 52, 70, 71, 80
Orkney 10, 16, 17, 29

peat 28
Peeblesshire 16, 59
Pentland Firth 14, 31
Perth, Perthshire 35, 66
Picts 10, 11, 12, 17, 31, 66, 72, 78, 85, 93
politics 81
Port Glasgow 53

Queensferry 55, 56

Reformation 21, 84
Renfrewshire 37, 78
Romans 9, 10, 17, 50
Ross-shire 28
Roxburghshire 36, 59, 90

St Andrew 83, 84
St Andrews 35, 67, 83, 84, 94
St Columba 12, 13, 33, 72, 87, 88, 93, 94
St Kentigern (Mungo) 50
St Kilda 27, 28, 31, 41
St Ninian 11, 12
Scots (tribe) 12, 13
Scott, Sir Walter 57, 59, 89–90
Scottish Office 73, 74
Selkirk 59
Shetland 13, 16, 17
ships 31, 32, 50, 51, 52, 53, 56, 71, 78, 92
ski-ing 27, 71
Solway 10, 13, 35
Spey, River 72
sport 71, 93, 94
steel 49, 78–9
Stevenson, Robert Louis 90–91
Stirling 17, 18, 32, 54, 55
Stone Age 7
Stone of Destiny 13, 38, 66
Stuart, Prince Charles Edward 22, 49, 73, 74
Sutherland 28

Tay, River 63, 64, 66, 67
television 38, 92, 93
Tweed, River 59, 60, 62

Union of the Crowns 20, 59
Union of Parliaments 21, 23
universities 50, 83

Wallace, William 17, 18, 48, 56
West Lothian 37, 78
whisky 52, 69, 79, 80
wool 60, 61